BAH! HUM-BUG!

101 Great Reasons to Hate the Holidays

by RON BARRETT & PATTY BROWN

A John Boswell Associates Book

POCKET BOOKS

New York London Toronto Sydney Tokyo Singapore

An *Original* Publication of POCKET BOOKS

POCKET BOOKS, a division of Simon & Schuster Inc.
1230 Avenue of the Americas, New York, NY 10020

ISBN: 0-671-79600-3

First Pocket Books trade paperback printing November 1992

10   9   8   7   6   5   4   3   2   1

POCKET and colophon are registered trademarks of
Simon & Schuster Inc.

Printed in the U.S.A.

1 The shopping day countdown now begins in July.

2 People who get their shopping done by mid-October

3 The one year you buy all your gifts early, you forget where you put them.

4 Thanksgiving, formerly a great holiday, is now a wholly owned subsidiary of Christmas.

5 Being too old to recognize any celebrities in the Thanksgiving Day Parade

6 Gifts ordered by mail in November are now due to arrive just in time for St. Patrick's Day.

① Mail order catalogs

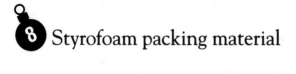

8 Styrofoam packing material

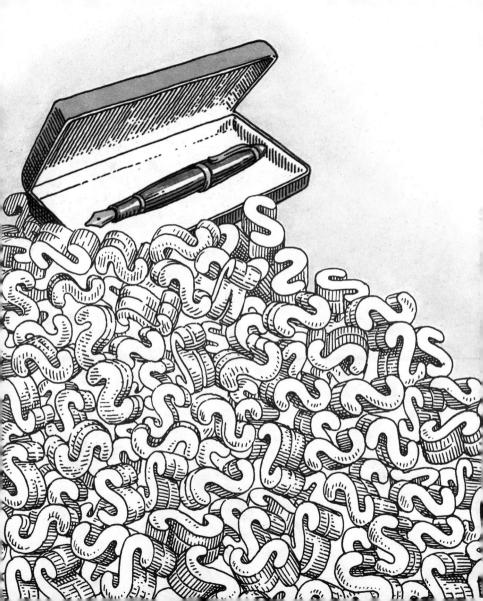

10 You are dressed for winter; the stores are thermostatically set at 103°.

 "Xmas"

14 Being a man in the women's underwear department

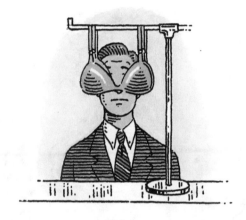

15 The overly made-up lady in the cosmetics department who sprays you with a perfume that makes you break out in hives

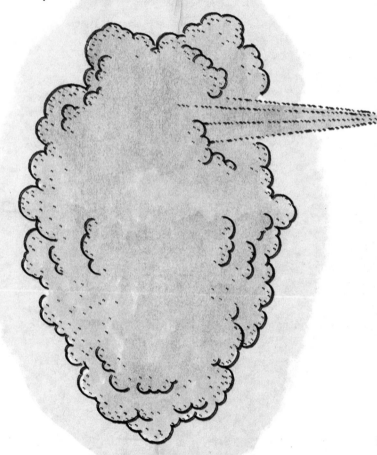

16 The store is open on the inside, but it's CLOSED to you on the outside.

17 Explaining that that's not *really* Santa, but one of his helpers

18 Santa openly suggests your child ask for some extravagant toy.

19 Knowing the tree you just paid $50 for would cost you $5 two weeks from now

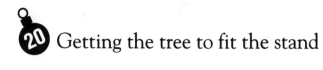

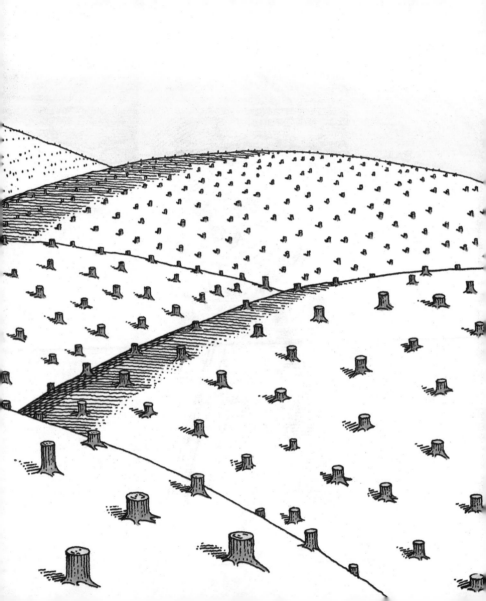

22 You can't find the box of Christmas stuff.

23 Your silk knee-length socks are the only ones big enough to hold all the candy.

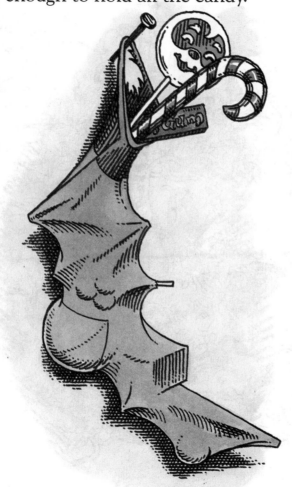

24 Locating the burned-out bulb on a string of tree lights

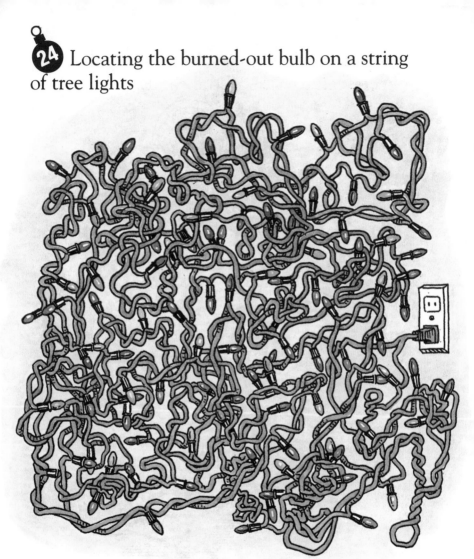

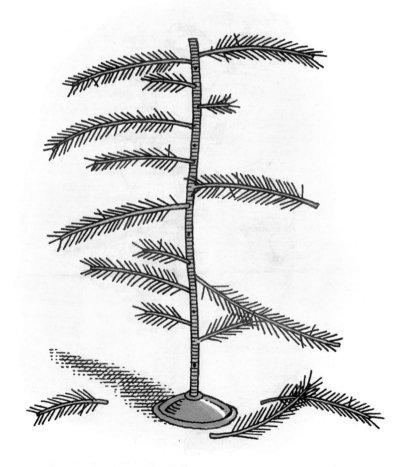

26 Trying to tie a bow with only two hands

27 One tiny sheet of wrapping paper wrapped around a giant cardboard tube

28 Paper cuts

29 Picking at a roll of transparent tape to find its end

30 Stepping with a bare foot upon a glass ornament

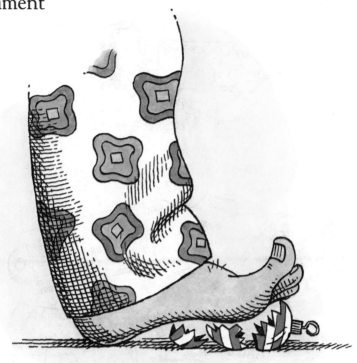

31 As a "Secret Santa" you have to buy a gift for someone you openly hate

32 What you get out of the office grab bag

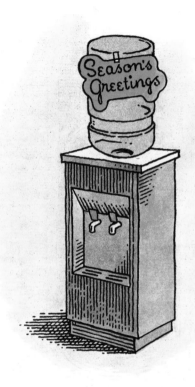

EGG ROLLS

PIZZA ROLLS

SHRIMP BALLS

CAULIFLOWER TEMPURA

MINIATURE POTATO KNISHES

CHEESE PUFFS

35 Mr. Dwiggins, who was a perfect gentleman before the office Christmas party, drops an olive down your blouse.

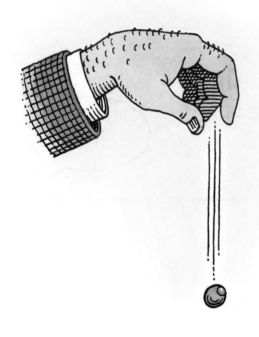

36 Having to face the person you did *that* with the day after the office Christmas party

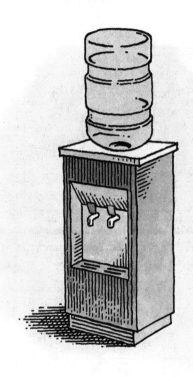

38 "In lieu of this year's Christmas bonus, the Company hopes this fine arts calendar brings you and your family a year of pleasure and cultural enrichment."

Nu Avec Cure-dents et Ordures / Nude With Toothpick and Litter *by Juan Gris*

JANUARY

		1	2	3	4	5
6	7	8	9	10	11	12
13	14	15	16	17	18	19
20	21	22	23	24	25	26
27	28	29	30	31		

39 The card from your supplier that reads: "We have made a donation in your name to our favorite charity" when you really could have used the money

40 Plastic mistletoe

The next-door neighbor going all out for top prize in the house-decorating contest

42 "Rudolph the Red-Nosed Reindeer" on every radio station

43 "It's a Wonderful Life" on every channel

44 In her ballet school's production of *The Nutcracker* your daughter is downgraded from a snowflake to a mouse.

45 Standing three hours at a school pageant to hear your child recite a four-second line in a chorus with forty other kids

FAMILY NEWSLETTER

❧ Christmas Issue ❧

As we gather with our families in the glow of hearth and holiday, let's remember the larger family of which we're all a part and how much there is to celebrate about it ∽

WELCOME BACK DAVE from drug rehab - out in time for the holidays with his folks. OOOPS! We mean <u>folk</u>! Dave's dad's been missing since July!

FINANCIAL PICTURE'S BRIGHT for Stacey! Her unemployment benefits have been e x t e n d e d ! ! !

UP THE LADDER! Let's hear it for Tiffany - she's been promoted from "topless" to "partially clothed" at Roy's Lord Squire Lounge!

HIGH TEST SCORE FOR DONNY! "*In the top percentile!*" said awed police of Donny's breathalyzer score. Test was given after Donny drove his Impala through the housewares section of a K-Mart.

OUR FAMILY'S FIRST GRAD SCHOOL GRAD, Kevin, has landed a job as assistant goatherd at the Great American Petting Zoo! Send Kev a card of congrats c/o Zoo, Century Mall, Thousand Oaks, CA

NEW ARRIVAL! 5 lb. Kendrick, born to Kimmy, who discovered her pregnancy only when she had her stomach emptied of the Old Spice she accidentally imbibed at a party!

BOLD CAREER MOVE FOR CHRIS! He's leaving high school to devote full time to curatorial work on his collection of nose hairs.

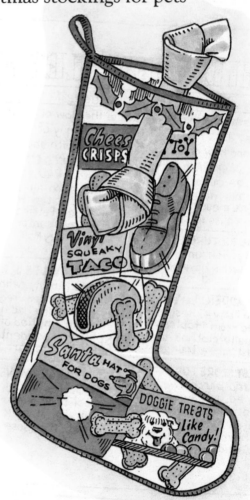

48 Grandma saying for the past twenty years, "Don't buy me anything, I'm going to die soon."

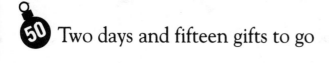

51 Remembering to put out Santa's milk and cookies, but then forgetting to eat them

52 Attempting to explain "he threw up the sash"

53 Explaining the mechanics of Santa's delivery system when you don't have a fireplace

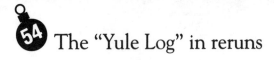

54 The "Yule Log" in reruns

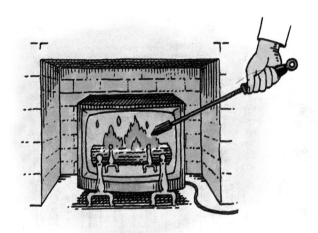

55 Any Christmas special hosted by Andy Williams, Perry Como, or John Denver

56 You've stayed up past midnight to wrap the children's gifts. They are up before dawn to open them.

57 Having to pretend you really like the
Gourmet Smoked Pork Butt and Cheese Log
Assortment

58 You open the wrong end the one time the label says "Open other end," and really means it.

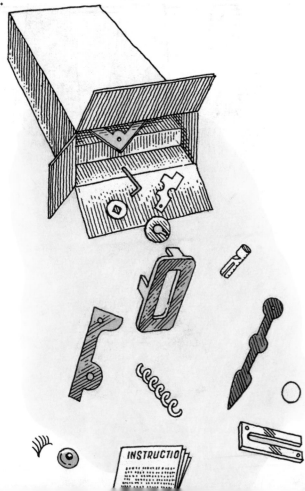

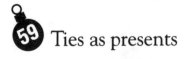 Ties as presents

THE CAUSE THE SCRIBBLE THE PROMOTIONAL

SAVE THE SQUID

Irish Whisky Makes Me Frisky

 Boxer shorts with candy canes on them

You find a pin in the gift shirt after you put it on.

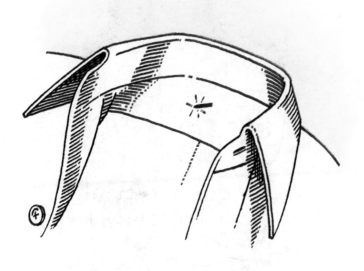

HIS HERS

MONET'S CLOSET

VESALIUS'
ANATOMICAL STUDIES
Coloring Book

COLOR THE ENGRAVINGS OF
THE GREAT RENAISSANCE
ANATOMIST!

The 24-Part
PBS Series
THE DULWIT
CHRONICLES

OGHAM
Rubber Stamps
USE THE ALPHABET
OF THE DRUIDS TO
COMPOSE YOUR OWN
GREETING CARDS,
PARTY INVITATIONS
AND PRAYERS TO
PAGAN DEITIES.

THE
ENCYCLOPEDIA
OF
PORCELAIN
BIRDS

THE SCRAMBLED
ÆNEID
The Mind-Boggling
Jigsaw Version
of Virgil's Famous
Epic Poem

67 The children are bored with their toys by 7:30 A.M.

68 By 7:35 A.M. the children's boredom turns into bitterness toward Santa.

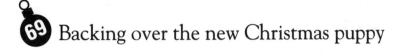

69 Backing over the new Christmas puppy

71 Candy canes that break into a million pieces

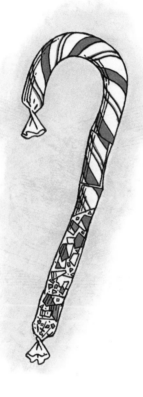

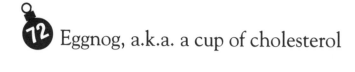

Egg Nog

Egg Nog

WARNING: THE
SURGEON GENERAL
HAS DETERMINED
THAT CONSUMPTION
OF THIS PRODUCT
RESULTS IN BLOCKAGE
OF CORONARY
ARTERIES AND
EXCESSIVE PHLEGM.

73 After five and a half hours at 375° the turkey is still frozen.

74 The turkey won't fit in the microwave.

75 Uncle Jack has three bourbons before dinner and tells that nurse joke again.

The dog has mounted the turkey.

77 Tough white meat and bones in a bag of burnt skin: It's either the overcooked turkey or Aunt Sadie up from Boca.

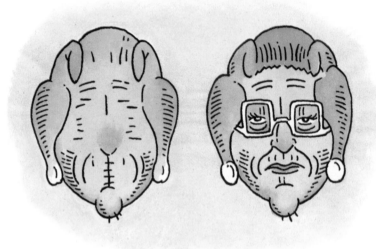

78 Having to explain to the kids why Bob called Ralph "his lover" at dinner

80 The person who gave your child the drum

 81 The drum instruction video

83 The irrationally pleasant airline clerk who tells you your flight has been canceled

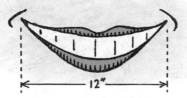

84 Finding out your flight is overbooked, and you are the overbookee

A family of four squeezed into two seats on an airplane and you're sitting next to them

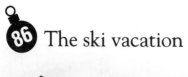

86 The ski vacation

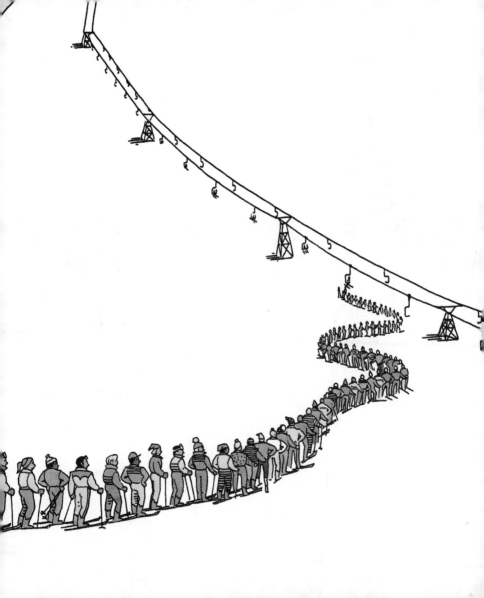

88 The psychologist on "The Today Show" who tells us we'll all be depressed in January

89 We're all depressed in January.

90 The guy who said "Just give the tree plenty of sugar and water and it won't shed"

Trying to fit a 75-gallon tree into a 50-gallon trash bag

The person who buys all of next year's cards and wrapping paper on December 26 at 50% off

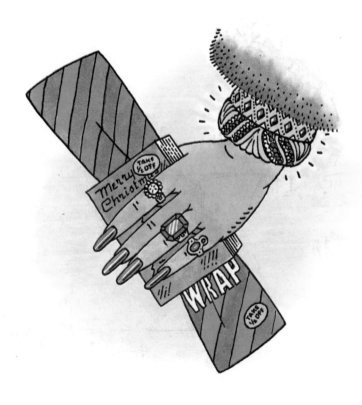

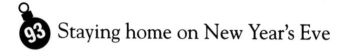

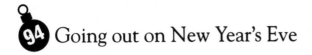

95 New Year's Eve parties have to last until midnight.

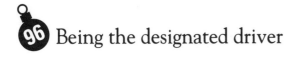

Being the designated driver

97 Trying to find your coat on the bed when you'd rather just lie on it

98 Trying to have a good time in a rented tuxedo

99 Starting the New Year with your head in the toilet

100 New Year's resolutions and the people who keep them

101 Your tip to the postman wasn't big enough.